That Face

Polly Stenham received both the Critics' Circle and the
Charles Wintour Award for Most Promising Playwright
for her first play, *That Face*, which opened at the Royal
Court Theatre and transferred to the West End. *That
Face* was also winner of the TMA for Best New Play,
2008. Her second play, *Tusk Tusk*, premiered at the
Royal Court Theatre in 2009.

POLLY STENHAM

That Face

faber and faber

First published in 2007
by Faber and Faber Limited
Bloomsbury House
74–77 Great Russell Street
London WC1B 3DA

This revised edition first published in 2008

Typeset by Country Setting, Kingsdown, Kent CT14 8ES
Printed and bound by CPI Group (UK) Ltd, Croydon, CR0 4YY

A CIP record for this book
is available from the British Library

ISBN 978-0-571-24421-8

8 10 9

For Cob
who's watching from the Gods

My favourite date,
much missed,
this one's for you

That Face was first presented at the Royal Court Jerwood Theatre Upstairs, London, on 20 April 2007. The cast was as follows:

Martha Lindsay Duncan
Mia Felicity Jones
Henry Matt Smith
Izzy Catherine Steadman
Hugh Julian Wadham
Alice Abigail Hood

Director Jeremy Herrin
Designer Mike Britton
Lighting Designer Natasha Chivers
Sound Designer Emma Laxton
Assistant Director Anna Dirckinck-Holmfeld

The production transferred to the Duke of York's Theatre, London, on 1 May 2008, presented by Sonia Friedman Productions, Tulchin/Bartner, Eric Abraham and Jamie Hendry, with Hannah Murray in the role of Mia and Rebecca Eve as Alice. The Assistant Director was Kate Lonergan.

SCENE ONE

A boarding school dorm late on a Sunday night. Alice is sitting on a chair. Her limbs have been tied to it. A black, beanie-style hat has been pulled over her face.

Mia Can she breathe?

Izzy Wait . . .

Izzy takes some scissors and cuts a hole in the hat. She makes the hole wider with her fingers. Alice's mouth can now be seen.

Just to be sure.

Mia Stick your tongue out.

Alice complies.

Wiggle it around.

Alice complies.

Roll it.

Alice complies.

I can't do that, you know. Look.

She tries to roll her tongue unsuccessfully.

Izzy Mia . . .

Mia You know, only some people can. It's like half. It's meant to be a sign of intelligence. Or something. Or maybe gayness. I can't remember. But look. No matter how hard I try . . .

Tries again.

Izzy MIA!

Mia Sorry. On the ball. I know.

Izzy Alice. Honey. Tonight is the night. You are to be . . . awakened.

Mia Like that. 'Awakened'. Nice.

Izzy It's a euphemism.

Mia I know.

Izzy As I was saying. Alice. Honey. Sweetie. Darling. Tonight is the night. Let's run through this again. Are you allowed to talk?

Alice shakes her head loosely.

Are you allowed to complain?

Shakes head.

Good girl. Isn't she a good girl, Mia?

Mia Wonderful.

Izzy Now. I would like as best as possible to keep this . . . clean, impersonal, professional, etcetera. But before we start the simulation, I would like to ask our . . . charge . . . a few mandatory questions. Which in this special instance she may answer.

Alice's head lolls.

Stay with me, Alice.

Her head jerks up.

Alice. In my short time as your head of dorm. I and Mia, your esteemed house sister.

Mia makes a mock curtsy.

Have noticed a small pendant hanging around your neck. Am I correct in believing this to be a religious symbol?

Alice nods.

A symbol of devout Christianity?

Alice nods slightly.

A cross, to be specific. Yes?

Alice does nothing.
    Mia grabs the back of Alice's head and nods her head for her.

Yeeess. Our suspicions were correct, esteemed house sister, deputy head of dorm and all things marvellous.

Mia Deputy. I've been promoted –

Izzy We're short-staffed. Alice. Honey. Sweetie. Darling. You have been observed over this first week and it has been concluded that you do, indeed, wear the aforementioned symbol all the time. Or should we say . . .

Beat.

Religiously.

Beat.

Answer please.

Alice nods her head very slightly.

That is sufficient. Did you note the response, Mia?

Mia Yes, sir.

Izzy There are no 'sirs' in this room. Mia – do you observe a single pair, or indeed a single testicle in this dorm?

Mia No.

Izzy Correct. So none of this 'sir' business. You may refer to me as esteemed head of dorm, high priestess or, if you prefer, more simply, God. Because. Need I remind you, Alice? Honey. Sweetie. I am your God.

Beat.

For tonight.

Beat.

So we had better take that thing off.

Izzy goes to remove the necklace. As she does so, Alice slumps forward.

Lazy fuck. Hold her up.

Mia struggles to pull Alice up by her shoulders.

Mia Heavy.

Izzy Fat.

Beat.

Mia/Izzy Misshapen death bat.

Izzy You sleepy, baby? Have we tired you out? Aw. Is it bedtime?

Mia loosens her grip on Alice. She slumps forward again.

Hold her up.

Mia I'm trying.

Izzy Alice? Stop pretending. You're making this tricky. And you wouldn't want to make this tricky now, would you? Would she, Mia? Would she be so silly as to pretend to be asleep? Silly things happen to silly girls now, Alice. Silly things . . .
Alice?

Izzy shakes her. No response.

You wouldn't want us to do it all over again tomorrow night now, would you?

Would you?

Izzy shoves her. No response.

Jesus, Mia.

She examines Alice.

What's wrong with her?

Shakes Alice vigorously.

She's out cold.

Mia I gave her some Valium.

Izzy You what?

Mia I. Gave. Her. Some. Valium.

Izzy I heard what you said.

Mia Well. Um. Sorry. I guess.

Izzy You gave her some Valium? You gave her a fucking tranquilliser . . . you . . . you . . . druggie.

How did you give it to her? Pop it in her tea? Slip it up her bottom while she was absorbed in *Neighbours*? Tell her it was a vitamin, a Smartie, an ecstasy pill? How did you give it to her, Mia?

Mia Well, I –

Izzy She had better be all right. If she's not we – correction, you – are in big trouble. Actually, correction, I am in big trouble, because I am head of dorm and you slipped our little house sister prescription drugs. She is basically my responsibility. Shit. Shit. Shit.

Mia Don't 'shit, shit, shit' me. Your responsibility is tied to a chair looking like a torture victim. I'd be more worried about that if I were you.

Izzy You know full well that that is different. This initiation. It's tradition. The teachers don't care. The sixth form don't care. It's practically goddamn allowed. Besides. It's meant to be fun.

Beat.

For us. Shit.

Mia Calm down.

Izzy Don't you dare tell me to calm down. We're screwed. Look at her. How many?

Mia What?

Izzy Pills? How many pills?

Mia In milligrams, I guess, forty. Maybe fifty. It was five tablets at ten each, so –

Izzy You are taking the piss. *Tell me* you are taking the piss. Even I know that's tons.

Mia Well, she's a big girl.

Izzy I hate you. I absolutely hate you. Look at her. She's un-fucking-conscious. We're screwed. They'll tell my parents. Shit shit shit.

Mia giggles.

Are you laughing at me?

Mia No.

Izzy You're laughing at me, aren't you? You fucking dare . . .

Mia Calm down. She'll be fine. I just, well . . . I thought it would help.

Izzy How, Mia, how did you think poisoning a thirteen-year-old girl would help? How? I'm dying to know.

Mia It's not poison. It's a mild tranquilliser . . . stops panic. Takes the edge off things. You can be nasty, when you get . . . you know, excited, and I wanted the initiation thing to go smoothly. I thought she'd be quieter. I thought you'd like that. You could do more to her.

Izzy Gee. What a gesture. How fucking considerate of you.

Beat.

Look at her.

Izzy tries to wake her. No response.

She's un-fucking-conscious.

Mia She's not unconscious, just super relaxed.

Izzy (*near tears*) This is it. We're screwed. I won't be a prefect, which will fuck up my UCAS, my mum . . . Oh God.

Mia snorts with laughter. Izzy spins around to face her.

Mia Sorry. It's just . . . the prefect thing.

Izzy Watch it.

Mia You're scared, aren't you?

Izzy No, I'm not. I'm realistic.

Mia God for the night, trembling in her pyjamas.

Izzy I am not scared.

Mia You're shaking. It's too much, isn't it? You only like good clean torture.

Izzy Fuck you.

Mia In your big wet dreams, scaredy-cat.

Izzy You little –

Mia What, little what?

Izzy Shit.

Mia Ooo . . . terrifying.

Izzy Shut up.

Mia I might collapse in fear.

Beat.

You're soft as a kitten, really. Aren't you?

Izzy Fuck you –

Mia As a baby's bottom. You just pretend –

Izzy SHUT UP.

Mia You just pretend. Really you have a heart of marshmallow –

Izzy Cocky –

Mia All gooey and sweet –

Izzy Cocky little –

Mia What? Cocky little what?

Beat.

Izzy (*snarls*) Shit.

She turns to Alice and yanks her head up.

(*Snarls.*) Cocky little shit.

She starts to circle Alice.

Mia Ooo, nasty.

Izzy Hold her up.

Mia Ooo, scary.

Izzy HOLD HER UP.

Beat.

This isn't over yet.

Mia Yes, sir.

She mock-salutes.

SCENE TWO

Monday morning. Flat in London.
Henry's bedroom. Neat, tidy, boyish. His photographs and drawings are pinned to the walls; some have been ripped down and torn as part of a struggle the night before. The ripped pictures contrast strongly with the order of the room.
Henry is asleep at the end of the bed, on top of the covers. He is wearing pyjamas. Martha is asleep inside the bed. She is wearing a nightdress.
Martha wakes up. She groans. She sits up, and then flops down again. She lies still, as if trying to get back to sleep. She then wriggles into a sitting position and lights a cigarette. She seems to be trying to remember the night before.
She watches the sleeping Henry. She leans forward and strokes his hair. She tries to arrange the duvet so it covers him.
She walks around the bed and regards Henry at all angles. She notices he still has his socks on. She slides them off.
She covers him more with the duvet.
She touches his hair. She strokes his face.
She leaves the room. Sounds of her banging around in the kitchen.
Henry stirs. He wriggles deeper into the bed.

Martha returns. She has washed her face and done up her nightdress. She is holding two mugs of coffee and a book.

She puts the coffee and the book down and sits next to Henry. She begins to stroke his back in long, slow, luxurious motions over his pyjama top.

Henry stirs and wriggles closer to her. Nestling into her warmth.

Martha Baby boy . . . So good.

Regards him. Continues stroking in silence.

Sorry.

Beat.

Sorry. Sorry. Sorry.

Beat.

Martha You look so handsome. Like a Russian soldier.

She starts to scratch his back, gently, in long strokes. Henry stretches out, still seemingly asleep, and makes a satisfied sound.

Soldier boy. So good.
Forgive me and I will be good. I promise. Never again. Henry . . . ?

Henry stirs. Beat.

Can we forget about it? Please.
I'll make it up to you.

He nods sleepily.

Was that a yes . . . ?

He nods again and stretches out to be scratched more. He wakes up properly. At first he is sleepy and disorientated. Then it dawns on him.

Henry Hungover.

Martha What?

Henry Are you hungover?

Martha I'm fine.

Beat.

I brought you some coffee. I thought we could go out and get some breakfast.

Henry I'm not hungry –

Martha A big fry-up. Anything you want.

Henry Surprise, surprise. No food in the house.

Martha I could go and get some.

Henry Do you even know where Waitrose is?

Martha You could have it in bed.

Henry I'm not hungry, and I bet you're feeling sick.

Martha I feel fine.

Henry You feel guilty.

Martha Please, Hen. I said I was sorry. I mean it. I really mean it. It won't happen again. I promise. What can I do to prove it to you?
Well, just you see. I will. It might take time, but I will.

She starts to stroke his back again.

Let's have a nice day together. We can do anything you want.

He flinches away from her stroking.

Henry Stop touching me like that. It's perverse.
You don't remember much, do you?

Martha I –

Henry I find that a sick justice. Whenever this happens, I wake up remembering it. Remembering everything you said, and you wake up weird and optimistic.

Martha Please –

Henry You can't really be sorry. Not if you don't properly remember.

Martha Don't be nasty to me, I beg you. Don't, Henry. Don't. I'm just trying to make it. Up. I won't do it again. We can clean the flat together. I wish I could take it – (*Gulp.*) – back. I don't think you understand – when you are older you'll understand. (*Gulp.*) Don't be cruel. I mean it. (*Sobs.*)

> *He watches her cry.*
> *She cries harder. He watches in silence.*
> *She starts to gasp. She starts to hyperventilate.*
> *He doesn't budge.*

What if you don't? If you don't, what will I do? You're all I have. What will I do? I love you. I'm not perfect, I love you. I will get better. Please, Hen, you're scaring me, you're frightening me, please. What will I do if you don't – You're all I have. My baby boy, my baby boy. (*Gasp.*) Scaring me.

> *Henry gets up. Exits.*
> *When he is gone her hyperventilation calms noticeably. When he re-enters it increases in volume and speed.*
> *Henry is now carrying a brown paper bag. Expertly and dispassionately he fixes it to her mouth. He starts breathing in a deep slow regular breaths and signals to her to do the same. She does and begins to calm.*
> *When she is breathing regularly he takes the bag away and gently lowers her back onto the bed. He*

*props her up. He fetches a glass of water and a single
pill. She takes it and gratefully gulps it down with the
water.*

Henry You shouldn't have coffee this early. You know it
doesn't help.

Beat.

I know you egged that on.
    I don't know if you could help egging it on. But I know
you did.
    Cruella.
    I should be the one having a panic attack. What would
you do if I did, huh?

*Henry convincingly mocks Martha's hyperventilation.
He increases it in speed and volume, then flops back
on the bed as if dead.
    He twitches a few times.
    Martha whimpers.
    Henry sits up.*

Sorry. Maybe that was cruel.

She curls up into the bed.

Mummy . . .

He tries to pull the duvet away from her. She clings to it.

OK. I'm sorry.
    Martha . . .

He curls round her on the bed and hugs her.

Are you my mummy?

She nods.

Take me home?

She nods.

Really promise. Really try.

OK?

Then I'm sorry. You're sorry. Let's call it quits. But this is the last time. I know I say it every time.

But I mean it.

Martha I do too.

Let's spend the morning in bed. Be lazy.

Henry Makes a change.

Martha arranges herself on his bed.

In here?

Martha Yur room's nicer. Better light.

They arrange themselves, Henry on the bed, Martha in it. Martha props up the pillows. Henry clears the rest of the glass and then reaches under the bed and pulls out a sketch pad and materials. Martha opens her book – a historical biography of Marie Antoinette. She is halfway through reading it.

Henry draws. Martha reads.

After a few moments, Martha stops reading and starts to watch Henry work. She puts her book down and takes the sketch pad from him.

If it's through a window, the perspective is going to be different. See? There is more of a gradient. And you have to think about the glass in the window. Are those patterns for stained glass?

Henry Not sure.

Martha If they are, and the window is divided up into little parts, it might diffract the view out the window differently – (*Adds to the sketch.*) See what I mean . . .

Henry Think so.

She does a quick rough sketch.

Sort of . . .

Adds to the sketch.

More like that?

She hands it back to him.

Martha You know what you're doing.

Goes back to her book.

This is good. Marie Antoinette knew her rights.

Henry She got executed.

Martha I would rather have led a short life of incomparable luxury and decadence than a long and boring one.

Henry That doesn't surprise me.

Martha If I was her and you were my little princeling, you would have had a fleet of white horses and an army of beautiful concubines. You wouldn't have complained.

He laughs.

Although you would have lasted till you were . . .

Flicks back in the book and checks.

About ten years old.
Sod the concubines, then.

Goes back to reading. The door buzzes.
Beat.
Door buzzes again.

Oh, ignore it. Probably Sonia or something.

Henry Did you pay her?

Door buzzes again.

Did you pay her for the last time?

Door buzzes again.

Jesus, Martha, you didn't, did you?

Martha I did. I bloody did. Ignore it.

Door buzzes in rapid, urgent blasts.

She'll go away.

Door buzzes in one long continual blast.

Henry (*sighs*) Is there any cash in the house?

Henry's phone beeps. He checks the message and laughs.

It's Mia, it's her, she's outside. Thank God. I thought we'd have Sonia's bruiser boyfriend to deal with again.

Martha Mia?

Henry Yes, Mia.

Martha Why? She should be at school. Why?

Henry I don't know.

Door buzzes again.

I'm letting her in.

Martha Why? Why's she here? Why?

Henry I don't know.

Martha Little shit.

Henry Please don't. It's too early for this.

Martha She can't stay here.

Henry Stop it. I'm going to buzz her in?

Beat.

Don't give me that, that . . . expression. I know you don't get on, but please be nice to her, or if you can't do that just don't be anything. OK?

Beat.

OK?

Martha It's just . . .

Henry What?

Martha She always interrupts, you know?

Henry She's your daughter, act like it.

Door buzzes again.

Martha She doesn't like me.

Henry She's fifteen. Just be nice, OK?

Martha She looks at me nasty.

Henry Jesus, Martha, can I let her in?

Martha She's not staying.

Henry presses a button. Mia's footsteps can be heard coming up the stairs.

Henry Please. Don't make a scene.

Mia enters.

Mia Hi.

Pause.

Martha (*stilted*) How are you?

Mia Been better.

Martha Oh.

Mia I had a horrible journey. You know, those days where everything seems to be working against you. Ticket machine doesn't work, train stops on the track for about half an hour, babies crying . . . all that, today. Should have been here earlier. Well, I would have been, you know what I mean.

Martha That's a big bag.

Mia Don't worry. I'm not here for long –

Martha There's not enough –

Mia Room. I know.

Henry It's a Monday. Shouldn't you be at school?

Mia shrugs.

Why are you in London? Did they let you out for the day?

Pause. She won't meet his eyes.

Mia?

Mia I've just come for the keys.

Henry What?

Mia The keys to the Docklands. The keys to Dad's flat. Will you give them to me?

Henry What's going on?

Mia She knows.

Henry You know?

Mia School called. Last night. They spoke to you.

Martha I don't remember.

Henry The phone. It did . . . That was your school?

Mia Yeah.

Henry She . . . you hung up, didn't you? Christ.

Martha I don't remember.

Mia You were pissed. I think they knew that. They called Dad.

Beat.

They called Dad in Hong Kong. He's flying over.

Martha Excellent. Daddio is flying over to take over. 'Bout fucking time. You lot exhaust me.

Mia He's flying over. To talk to the school.

Henry What?

Mia He's leaving tonight.

Martha You spoke to him?

Mia Briefly.

Martha And how was the darling man?

Mia Brief.

Beat.

You should have these back.

She chucks a bottle of pills on the bed.

Henry You took them from here?

Mia Sorry.

Beat.

Sod that. I'm not. I've been sorry all night. Enough with being sorry.

Martha You took my pills?

Mia Yep.

Martha I need these pills. My doctor gave me these pills.

Mia I know, Mum, Martha, whatever.

Martha Don't be cheeky.

Mia That's not what I meant. I meant 'whatever' as in whatever your name is, whatever I'm meant to call you. Not 'whatever' as in I don't care . . . I do care.

Beat.

Those are ridiculous pyjamas.

Martha You stole these.

Henry Leave it, Martha.

Martha What would have happened if I'd needed them, eh? She stole them from me. On purpose.

Mia You have more. It's not as though you don't have more.

Martha How do you know that, Missy?

Mia You don't exactly hide your prescription stash.

Martha See. See. She's always rude to me. She steals from me. She has no –

Henry Leave it. Both of you.

Heavy pause.

Martha (*getting up to go, mutters*) Always interrupting.

She exits.
  Sound of water running and door closing.
  Mia flops down on the bed, exhausted.

Henry He's coming over?

Mia Just get me the keys, Henry.

Henry Why? Why's he coming?

Mia Please. Just go and get them.

Henry What's going on?

Mia is fingering some of Henry's drawings.

Mia This is good, you know. I think you're getting better.

Henry You're either sick, or you're in trouble. And you don't look sick.

Mia I think I saw one of your paintings by the station. Did you do one there? On the wall behind the car park?

Henry You're in trouble, aren't you? You did something.

Beat.

And you don't look sick.

Mia It was really pretty.

Henry Mia?

Mia I wish you'd draw me.

Henry Why did they call?

Mia Just get me the keys. Henry.

Henry Not until you tell me.

Mia Fine. I'll find them.

Henry Mia, spit it out.

Mia You don't. You won't. You don't want to know. You'll hate me.

Henry I could never hate you.

Mia (*almost to herself*) What are they going to do to me . . . ?

Henry Who?

Mia The school, you fool. They're going to expel me, Hen. I just know they are. And Dad. Oh God.

Henry Mia. I don't care. I won't hate you. I promise I won't. I promise. Just tell me.

Mia (*into the pillows*) Fuck. Fuck. Fuck.

Henry Whatever it is. Whatever you've done. I'll support, I'll stand by you. I promise.

Mia You really promise?

Henry Promise. What was it? The pills. You tried to sell the pills at school or something?

Mia Sell them? No. I didn't think of that. Though I could have made a fortune. They're all loaded. Could have flogged them round exam time when everyone's stressed.

Henry That's not funny.

Mia I wasn't trying to be.

Henry Tell me.

Mia It was something that started as fun and ended up . . .

Beat.

Serious.

Henry It must be serious if Dad's planning to show his face. So you didn't sell them. You took them? What?

Mia I . . .

Henry What?

Mia I gave them to a younger girl.

Henry OK. Right. How old?

Mia Thirteen.

Henry *Mia!*

Mia You said you wouldn't be angry.

Henry OK. Sorry. Is that it? Is that all?

Mia Sort of.

Henry What do you mean, sort of?

Mia I gave her rather a lot.

Henry How many?

Mia Forty mills.

Henry You're joking. Even Martha couldn't handle that. Fuck.

Mia I didn't realise.

Henry You know the dosage. That's tons, Mia.

Mia No. You know the dosage.

Henry Of course you do. You've given them to her before.

Mia No. You always do. She never wants me to.

Henry What happened? After you gave them to the girl? What happened to the girl?

Mia She sort of fell asleep.

Henry Passed out.

Mia No. She did wake up at one point. She was just tranquillised really. Slower. Quieter.

Henry She told on you?

Mia Not exactly. We sort of told on ourselves. Well. It was obvious. What we'd done. Besides. We couldn't lie. They found it in her bloodstream.

Henry *What?*

Mia She's in hospital.

Henry You're joking. This is an exeat, and you're joking.

Mia I wish I was.

Henry Oh, Mia. Oh God.

Mia I'm sorry. I . . . I'm sorry.

Henry And he's coming over? Definitely?

Mia Definitely.

Henry Oh, Mia. How could you?

Mia Don't.

Henry Why does he have to be involved? Why didn't they call me? I could have come. They know me. I always drop you off.

Mia I told you. They did call.

Henry I should have got to the phone. Shit. Why didn't they call my mobile? I gave that number to your house mistress. For emergencies. Why didn't they call that?

Mia After speaking to Martha, they decided they were 'concerned' about my domestic situation. She must have been smashed. The look on their faces was priceless. God knows what she said. They had to call Dad. You're barely eighteen, Henry, you're not old enough.

Henry She was in a state last night. Angry at everything. Everyone.

Mia Well she's hung herself this time. 'Who looks after you in the holiday, Mia?' 'How regularly is your mother like that, Mia?' 'Since when have you had access to your Mother's drugs. Mia?' Bla bla bla.

Henry What did you say?

Mia The truth. That I barely lived here, just bummed at friends' houses mostly, or the Docklands place.

Henry This is bad.

Mia I know.

Henry This couldn't have happened at a worse time. She's getting better. See how she left before getting nasty. She's learning some self-control.

Mia Dream on, Henry. I've heard it all before. Just get me the keys, OK?

Martha (*from offstage*) HENRY!

Henry WHAT?

Martha FORGOT MY TOWEL.

Henry finds one and exits to give it to her. While he's gone Mia begins to smoke one of Martha's cigarettes. Henry re-enters.

Henry 'We'. You said 'we'. Who else was involved?

Mia Another girl. Izzy.

Henry Older?

Mia Year above.

Henry Which hospital is she in?

Mia They moved her to a London one this morning. The Portland.

Henry You have to go there.

Mia Go there?

Henry Go there and find the girl. Talk to her. Apologise. Convince her to say it was all Izzy. That Izzy, um . . . coerced you into it.

Mia What's the point?

Henry Then Dad won't have to get too involved. He knows Martha's a prescription popper anyway. If he thinks it wasn't so much you –

Mia Because I'm clearly such an innocent lamb.

Henry If the school think it wasn't so much you, he'll just throw a bit of cash at the school and fuck right off. I don't want him to come here.

Mia It won't work.

Henry It might. You've got to. You've got to try. He can't come here.

Mia Come with me.

Henry You know I can't.

Mia Why?

Henry If I'm around she won't drink today. She feels too guilty.

Mia Please. I want to go before she gets out. This place gives me the creeps.

Henry Hey . . .

Mia Sorry. But you know what I mean. It used to be nice. It should be nice. It's just so weirdly squalid now. Ugh.

Henry You'll be fine. Come straight back after.

Pause.

Mia You promised, Henry.

Pause.

Henry OK. Wait. My phone.

He shoves on some clothes.

Mia Docklands keys, Henry.

Henry In there.

She finds the keys and jangles them.

Mia Come on!

Henry My phone –

He goes to grab his phone.

Mia Sod that. You want to be free as a birdie. We could make a day of it. Hospital in the morning. Millennium Wheel in the afternoon.

Henry What if . . .?

Mia Pussy.

Henry But seriously, if . . .

Mia Mummy's boy.

Henry Fine.

He scribbles Martha a quick note and leaves it on the bed.
He gives his sister a playful push towards the door. She pushes him playfully back. He exits ahead of her.
While he can't see, she pockets the note he left for Martha.
Mia exits.

Martha (*from offstage*) HENRY!

Martha re-enters. Soaking wet in a towel.

HENRY!

SCENE THREE

Later that day. A private hospital room. Alice is in the hospital bed, her head partially swathed in bandages, and hooked up to a drip. It is not clear whether she is sedated, unconscious or asleep. Henry and Mia stand on either side of her. Mia is peering at Alice.

Mia Say something. Something. Please.

Beat.

She looks bad, doesn't she?

Henry Jesus, Mia.

Mia She's only wired up to this. Is that good?

Henry This is frightening. You know that. You are frightening.

Mia Don't.

Henry Don't what? What do you want me to say? That it's fine. You could have told me. Prepared me. Fuck. What had she done to you?

Mia It's not that . . .

Henry What? 'Not that' what?

Mia Simple.

Henry It is that fucking simple. You don't go around doing that to people. You just don't.

Mia You don't understand.

Henry No. You're right. I don't.

Mia In the context, what happened, what we were doing. It seemed OK. It seemed perfectly fine – allowed, even.

Henry All right? *This* seemed all right –?

Mia It's different in there: different rules, different power levels . . . it's messed up. Back in school, at night, when all the teachers are in bed and the power shifts . . . when age becomes like a rank. And people are bored.

Henry You can't excuse this, Mia. Nothing can excuse this –

Mia It's a different world, with different rules. And some stuff . . . well, it seems OK. Allowed even. But in the light of day, here. Before that, even, soon as I walked out of the gates and saw normal people, no uniform. Then I realised how messed up it was, what happened. But when I was in the dorm, with Izzy, tying her up – well, I could only see the particles, the teeny tiny particles. Not the whole picture.

Henry You frighten me.

Mia Should I try and apologise?

Henry What if we're seen?

Mia It was your idea.

Henry I didn't know how bad this was, did I? If I'd have known –

Mia Alice . . .

Henry Let's just go.

Mia Relax, her parents don't know what we look like.

Henry They probably do now.

Mia They dropped her off early at the start of term. So we never met.

   Beat.

I've seen photos, though . . . by her bed. They looked nice.

   Henry fingers some paper cups by the side of the bed.

Henry Jesus, Mia. These are still warm.

Mia (*distracted*) So they've just left.

Henry So they've gone to get more coffee. I think we should go.

Mia It was your idea.

Henry Because I thought she'd be propped up in bed feeling a bit woozy. Not. Not. Looking like a war victim. Jesus, Mia.

Mia But our plan –

Henry Is defunct. Let's go.

Mia (*distracted*) Have you seen the size of this?

She is examining a bruise on Alice's face.

It's massive.

Henry Please. Let's go. This is freaking me out. Besides, she could wake up.

Mia I thought you wanted her to wake up?

Henry How many times? This is different to what I thought. This is entirely different. Jesus. If she wakes up and sees you hovering here she'll probably scream. I would. Sod the plan. Let's go.

They both hear the sudden sound of someone knocking on the door. Scared, they hide under the bed.
Izzy enters, sniffling. She is holding an enormous, extravagant bunch of flowers and a grotesque hand-made card. She relaxes as soon as she realises the room is empty of visitors. She puts the flowers down on the foot of the bed. She walks up to Alice and peers at her.

Izzy (*softly*) Alice? Honey?

She tugs at her shoulder gently, no response. Tries again. No response.
Pause.
She flicks her face lightly with her finger. No response. She repeats the action harder. No response.
Satisfied that Alice is unconscious she begins to take in her own handiwork and lets out a low wolf whistle.

Alice, honey, you're a state . . .

Mia and Henry sneak out behind Izzy. Mia puts her hand over Izzy's mouth. Izzy shrieks.

Mia Shhh . . .

Izzy It's you. You scared me.

Beat.

Was it you two in here before?

Mia Yeah.

Izzy God, you got me all riled up. I thought it was the parents. I was exploiting my hay fever to the maximum.

She looks around the room.

Not bad, eh? She must have had insurance.

Mia Shhh . . . you might wake her.

Izzy Relax. She's out cold.

Mia Or pretending to be.

Izzy (*overly sweet*) Alice? Honey?

No response.

Henry Stop it.

Izzy Why are you here, then? To apologise? Spare me . . .

Izzy grins at Henry and Mia. she leans over and tweaks Alice's nipple. No response.

Told you. She's out of it.

Izzy sticks out her hand.

Izzy.

Henry I know.

Izzy Henry, right? Mia talks about you a lot. I hear you're an artist?

Mia has just noticed the flowers.

Mia You brought her flowers?

Izzy She told me you quit school to be a painter. I think that's sooo –

Mia And a card –

Izzy – cool, you know? I like to paint as well. I made this card. Look.

Henry Why bother?

Izzy Mummy thought it would be appropriate to offer my deepest sympathy. Besides, it's not going to hurt.

Mia She looks bad, doesn't she? I didn't remember her looking that bad.

Izzy You seem to forget what we did to her in the last twenty minutes.

    Beat.

Besides, bruises take time to swell and change colour. Haven't you ever had a black eye?

Mia A lax ball in the face.

Izzy Crap at catching.

Henry And I suppose she was crap at catching too?

Izzy She was just . . . crap.

Henry That's a horrible thing to say.

Izzy Lots of true things are.

    Both girls peer closely at the bruise.

Mia Who gave her that? You or me?

Izzy Which would you prefer?

Mia You.

Izzy Then it was me.

    Henry is guarding the door, facing away from the girls. Izzy checks him out.

So how come you're here?

Mia He's supporting me.

Izzy That's so sweet.

Henry I think we should go now, Mia.

Izzy She can sign the card if you want . . . (*Beat.*) I like your T-shirt.

Sound of footsteps approaching and a hospital trolley passing the door.

Mia They might come back with medicine or something.

Izzy Good idea. Let's go for a drink.

Mia Won't your mum want you back or something?

Izzy (*while arranging the flowers neatly by the bed*) Stuff it, I'm in so much trouble already it hardly matters if I get in a bit more. What can they do? Yell? I think Mummy's yelled herself out of oxygen.

Pause.

Come on. Let's go to the pub. Let's go . . . somewhere.

Beat.

What's with the faces? We should be celebrating. She's not nearly as bad as we thought.

Mia As you thought.

Izzy gives Alice another glance. She picks up the clipboard at the end of the bed and strikes a comic, learned, doctorly pose.

Izzy She's not dead. She's not about to die. So we're fine. Let's go toast to tough little Alice. Come on.

She saunters offstage, throwing a backward glance at Henry.

Come on.

She exits.

Mia She fancies you.

Henry She scares me.

They exit.
Alice shifts in her bed and begins to cry.

SCENE FOUR

Tuesday morning. Martha's flat. Henry's bedroom.
Martha is in his bed. There is an overflowing ashtray next
to the bed – it should look as though she's been camping
there all night.
Sound of Henry opening the door.

Martha Henry?

She gets out of bed.

Henry? HENRY?

Sound of a shower running.
Martha sits back down. She stands up. Sits back
down. She is clearly disconcerted. She goes to stand by
the door. She goes to leave the room, but at the last
minute thinks better of it and returns to the bed. She
gets in the bed, sitting up. She wriggles further down
into the bed. She pulls the duvet over her head. Stays
like this for a while.
Martha sighs. Water is still running. She sits up
again. Opens a book. Tries to read nonchalantly. Can't
focus. Finds a cigarette. Smokes it nervously. The shower
sound stops. She hurriedly puts it out, dives into the
bed and covers her body and head with the duvet.

Henry (*offstage*) Martha? Where are the clean clothes?
My shirts. I washed them. I strung them up in the . . .

They're not here . . .

Beat. Henry enters, dripping wet with only a towel around his waist. He searches his room for his clothes and can't find them.

Where are all my clothes?

Martha wriggles further down into the bed.

Where are they?
MUMMY.
Where are they?

She sits up.

Thank you.

They stare at each other. She looks at his upper body. She notices a love bite on his neck.

Give me something to put on.

Beat.

If you're not going to tell me where they are, I'll find something temporary.
Don't look at me like that.

Martha Why not?

Henry You know.

Beat.

Where are my clothes?

She stares at him.

Fine. Fine. I'll wear . . . I'll wear . . . this.

He holds up one of Martha's dressing gowns, a long white one with a flower design.
Martha moves towards the edge of the bed closest to him and sits on it.

Martha You're wet.

He turns away from her. There are scratches on his back. He chastely slips on the dressing gown and only when he's covered drops the towel. He ties the cord tightly.

Martha laughs at the sight of him. He smiles, shrugs and stares down at himself.

Your hair is wet.

He rubs his hair with the towel.

You could have worn what you came home in.

Henry It was dirty.

Beat.

Martha You're dirty. What's that on your neck?

Henry (*as if to a deaf person*) Where – are – my – clothes?
Mummy? MARTHA?

Martha (*as if to a deaf person*) Where – was – my – son?

Henry This isn't funny.

Martha Tit for tat. Tit for tit. I'll tell you if you tell me. Where were you?

Henry Out.

Martha Who with?

Henry Friends.

Martha You don't have any friends.

Henry You don't know everything about –

Martha About you, I do. You don't have any friends. You never had any friends.

Henry I was at a friend's flat. I missed the last bus. Where are my clothes?

Martha Who?

Henry Who?

Martha Who was your friend?

Henry A . . . a . . . mate, OK? Someone I used to know.

Martha Called?

Henry None of your business.

Martha Don't get cheeky. I'm your mother, not one of your . . . mates. What was the name?

Henry (*searching*) Ian.

Martha A boy.

Henry Yes. A boy.

Martha You stayed the night, with, a, boy?

Henry Two boys.

She starts to laugh.

Martha Come here.

She opens her arms. He approaches her warily. She hugs him.

Beautiful boy. Beautiful baby, covered in marks. You silly thing.

Rocks him.

You could have told me. But then, I think I always knew. I don't mind . . . I know some parents mind. My parents would have really minded. God . . . my father. But they were religious, and, not as close as us, eh? No. I don't mind a bit. I just don't want any secrets between us.

Beautiful boy. Russian soldier. You have to tell me all about it – not the details mind. But we can have a gossip. To be honest, I was starting to suspect, you being so gentle. So sweet. So utterly unlike any . . . Modern times, though, modern times –

Henry has reached into the bedclothes and pulled out a strip of cut-up shirt material.

Henry Jesus Christ.

He reaches in again and pulls out a handful. He springs up.

Get up.

She sits frozen.

GET UP.

She stands. Henry yanks the duvet from the bed. Revealed are a pile of his clothes, all cut up into teeny tiny strips. Henry climbs onto the bed. He picks up handfuls of the material. He starts to laugh. Martha, nervous, starts laughing too.

You – (*Laughs.*) You – (*Laughs.*) You – (*Laughs.*) crazy – (*Laughs.*)

Beat.

– bitch. You crazy bitch.

Martha It doesn't matter, does it? I'll buy you more. I just. Had. A moment. Last night. I was angry with you. You disappeared.

Henry Crazy –

Martha You disappeared and you didn't –

Henry – BITCH.

Silence.

Martha Sorry.

Sorry. Sorry. Please.

It's OK now. See? It's OK. Now I know where you were. So it's OK. Now I know what you are. It's OK. I just . . . No secrets. I can't bear it. Please.

Henry What am I, Martha?

Martha With men. You like men.

Henry laughs.

Henry You'd love that, wouldn't you?

Martha I love you. Whatever you are.

Henry I was with a girl. (*As if to a deaf person.*) I – was – sleeping – with – a – GIRL.

That's where I was. I didn't come home last night because I was with a woman. And that's where I wanted to be. With her. Not here. I could have come home but I didn't. Did you hear that? That is what I am. Just a little bit normal.

Beat.

That changes things, doesn't it?

You don't like that so much.

But remember. You love me.

Beat.

Whatever.

Martha Take it off.

Henry What?

Martha My dressing gown. Take it off. It's mine. I want it back.

Henry No. Sew me an outfit and I'll take it off. Stitch my clothes back together and I'll take it off. Behave like a remotely attractive human being and I'll take it off.

47

Martha Was that . . .

Henry What?

Martha Was that your first time?

Henry Yes.

Martha Oh.

Henry It had to happen. It was going to happen.

Martha I just thought. That. You didn't like women.

Henry You thought I liked men.

Martha No. Yes. No. I don't know.
   You're an artist. You're a gentle, perfect son. You're . . .
pretty. It made sense.

Henry Well. You clearly don't know me so well after all.

Martha It's. Just. A shock.

Henry That I'm straight? God. You live in an upside-
down world, Martha. Look. It wasn't to hurt you. I had
to do something for me. Don't you see?

Martha You're not mine any more. You're hers.

Henry I'm always yours. But I'm mine as well.

Martha Did she hurt you. Your back?

Henry You should have seen her.
   I'm joking.

Martha Why didn't you call? I got. Panicky.

Henry I was busy. Doing things. Doing things I should
be doing. Don't make me feel like . . . like it's wrong. I'm
your child, not –

Martha Russian –

Henry I know. Russian soldier. Whatever. Just let me go
a bit, please. This is crazy behaviour.

Martha Are you clean now?

Henry I showered.

Martha You don't smell? You know. Of another –

Henry Person. No, Mummy.

Martha Come here.

He goes to her. She smells him and strokes his hair. She hugs him tightly. She starts to open the front of the dressing gown.

Henry What are you doing?

Martha I want to see you.

Henry Christ. Why?

Martha Your body. I want to see if you look different. If you feel different. (*Urgently.*) Please. I need to. You're *my* child.

She smells his chest and buries her head in it. He sighs and wraps his arms around her, rocking her slightly. She presses the love bite with her fingers.

Does it hurt?

Henry No.

Martha Is she pretty?

Henry Yes.

Martha Will you see her again?

Henry Maybe.

She buries her head in his chest again. He wraps his arms around her and rocks her. They stay like this for a few moments. Suddenly Henry springs back. And shoves Martha away.
There is now another love bite on his neck.

Martha is smiling.

Martha When you do. You can show her that.

Blackout.

SCENE FIVE

Hugh's flat at Canary Wharf. It is minimalist and impersonal. A businessman's bachelor flat. It is his crash pad for his rare and increasingly infrequent visits to London. The flat is filled with light from large glass windows. There is evidence of a small drunken party: an iPod attached to speakers, an empty vodka bottle, some beer cans, a crammed ashtray, a twister board – all of these inconsistent with the overall design of the flat. There is also a large stain on the carpet.

    Mia walks in, dishevelled – she has just woken up. She is ending a call on her mobile phone, having just been talking to Hugh. She takes in the state of the room, the stain on the floor . . .

Mia Bugger.

She begins manically to tidy the flat.

Izzy! Henry! Guys . . .
    GET UP. Dad just called. He's landed. Izzy. IZZY! Come on. You have to go.

Izzy stumbles out of the bedroom, wrapped in a sheet. She flops onto the sofa. Mia yanks at the sheet.

Get dressed. You have to leave.
    HENRY . . .

Izzy Ouch. Stop shouting. My head hurts.

Mia HENRY! COME ON.

Izzy He's not here.

Mia What?

Izzy He left. Earlier.

Mia To go where?

Izzy Probably to buy some milk or something. Chill.

Mia Get dressed, Izzy, you have to go. (*Yanks at sheet.*)
Now.

Izzy Hey . . . I'm naked, you brazen hussy. Stop. Yanking.
What? Want a bit of me too?

Mia Get up.

Izzy Your brother loved it . . .

Mia Ugh. Ugh. That is so . . . disgusting. I don't want to
know.

Izzy I think we have a connection, you know. A special
connection. It's like we understand each other. Mentally . . .
spiritually . . .

*She really enjoys saying this, knowing it winds Mia up.
She mock-humps the air.*

Physically . . .

Mia Izzy. You disgust me. (*Mocking.*) Mentally,
spiritually . . .

She finds pants on the floor.

Ugh . . . physically. You can have *these* back.

Izzy catches the pants and dangles them on her finger.

Izzy Ripped them off me. Like an animal. He's gorgeous.
So . . . manly –

Mia (*snorts*) Manly?

Izzy So . . . commanding. Like I said, I think we have a
connection. I noticed it as soon as we met. It . . . it . . .
crackled with intensity . . . could you tell?

Mia Izzy, get off your arse and help me. Dad's gonna be here in like an hour. Look at this stain, he's going to kill me . . .

Izzy's mobile phone beeps.

Izzy Ah ha . . . It's from him . . . listen . . . 'To my darling cat' – we have nicknames – 'I can't stop thinking about you. Our night of passionate coupling –'

Mia Coupling?

Izzy So? He's old school. Listen: 'Our night of passionate coupling has blown me away and I'm lusting –'

Mia Ugh! Stop. It's wrong –

Izzy 'LUSTING after your bendy body' – 'bendy', eh? Knew the yoga was worth it. 'Your velvety skin . . .'

Mia interrupts her by jumping on her and beating her with a sofa cushion.

Mia Stop it stop it stop it. It's just wrong. Let me see that.

She tussles with Izzy for the mobile phone.

Izzy (*in mock sleazy Italian, waving the phone tauntingly at Mia*) What? You no like my velvety body? You no want to touch . . . to – how shall we say? – to *penetrate* –

Mia GROSS! I'm deleting that.

She grabs the phone and reads the text, then starts to laugh.

'Where are you, darling? We are so worried. Please call home.'

Mia starts giggling and hitting Izzy harder with the pillow.

Get. Up. You sad, dirty fiend. You have. To. Go.

Izzy (*still in mock sleazy Italian*) You no want my *bendy* body . . . Why? Is so good . . .

Henry enters, wild-eyed.
Izzy sits bolt upright, shoves Mia off her onto the floor, tosses her hair back and attempts to strike a sexy pose . . .

Mia You bitch, I thwacked my knee.

Izzy Hey you . . .

Mia Dad called. He's landed. He's on his way.

Izzy Well, I'm going to have a shower . . . Henry?

Henry How long will it take him to get here?

Mia I dunno. An hour maybe.

Izzy I'm *going* to have a shower . . . Honey?

Mia You don't have time, Izzy. You have to leave –

Izzy Don't you want to come in with me, baby . . . ?

Henry Huh? Oh. No thanks. I have to talk to Mia.

Izzy You don't know what you're missing.

She flounces out.

Mia You must be some stallion, Hen, she's besotted. (*Mocks Izzy.*) 'Come in the shower with me, baby.'

She starts scrubbing the stain on the floor.
Henry is wildly on edge. Mia doesn't notice.

Mia What is this stuff? It looks like wine, did we have wine? I can't –

Henry MIA!

She looks up and notices his wild eyes. She stops what she is doing.

Mia You went back, didn't you?

Henry nods.

Stupid . . .

Henry shakes his head softly. He looks as though he's about to cry or scream.

Hey. Henry. Hey.

Henry She's . . . gone.

Mia She left?

Henry No. She, Mum, real her, gone. She's gone.

Mia What do you –

Henry Eaten up. It's eaten her up. Like body-snatchers. Not her. That woman. It's not her . . .

Mia What did she say?

Henry (*to himself*) I don't know what to do. I just don't know what to do . . .

Mia Listen, Dad's on his way –

Izzy flounces back in, oblivious to Henry's state of mind and the nature of the conversation they've been having.

Izzy, you have to go.

Izzy (*to Henry*) I'm wearing your jumper, I hope you don't mind . . .

Mia NOW, Izzy.

Izzy It's all I could find. Henry, I was thinking, if you're free later –

Mia My dad is on his way back. Now. In a car, driving here. What part of that don't you understand? You have to go. NOW.

Izzy Well, you don't have to be so rude about it.

She gropes around the room for her clothes.

(*Mutters.*) Can't find my bra.

Mia finds it and chucks it at her.

Mia Go.

Izzy You don't have to be a moody cow about it. Respect your elders, sweetie.

Henry And you respect yours. Get the fuck out.

Heavy pause.
Izzy looks as if she's about to cry. She opens her mouth as if to say something but doesn't. She exits.

Mia Holy moly. I don't think she'll be angling for another round now. That was harsh, stud muffin.

Henry doesn't smile.

Oh Henry . . . Look, whatever she said, it doesn't matter now. Dad's on his way. He wants us to wait for him here. He said he's been doing a lot of thinking. He's says he's going to sort it out.

Henry (*to himself*) Daddio's on his way . . . . . . to save the day . . .

Mia The school . . . everything. He had that determined voice, you know? He said it, and you know what? I believe him.

Henry shakes his head.

Mia He's different, Henry. He wants to help.

Henry How graceful of him –

Mia Don't. Just give him a chance.

Henry He had his chance

Mia He waited for you at those restaurants. All those meals. You never came. He wanted you to. He tried, Henry –

Henry You're taking his side now –

Mia I was there. (*Gentler.*) He's got a plan.

Henry (*quietly*) He's got a plan?

Mia A strategy.

Henry (*quieter still*) A strategy.

Mia (*oblivious to the dangerous edge in Henry's voice*) It's going to end. Don't you see? Soon as he's here, he's going to take over, so you don't have to worry –

Henry I don't have to worry.

Mia He said . . . Look, I told him stuff, Henry. Not everything, but I will, I'm going to tell him tonight.

Henry (*quiet and dangerous*) You can't do that.

Mia You tried. You really tried, and I'll always love you for that. But she's worse. You can't handle it. Look at the state of you . . .

Henry Five years –

Mia – are over . . .

Henry That's easy for you to say. You didn't do anything. You didn't do anything for her.

Mia That's not fair.

Henry (*hisses*) Not fair? Not FAIR? You wouldn't know the meaning of unfair.

Mia Henry, please –

Henry Unfair is every other day, thinking maybe, just maybe, you're getting somewhere, that it's worth it –

Mia Henry, don't –

Henry (*quietly, almost to himself*) This has been my life. She has been my life.

Mia I know, and that's why we –

Henry (*livid*) YOU DON'T KNOW. NEITHER OF YOU KNOW. NEITHER OF YOU HAVE DONE SHIT.

Pause.

Mia If you left, Henry, it would settle, one way or another.

Henry What exactly do you mean?

Mia She'd top herself or get better.

Henry And let me guess which you'd prefer . . .

Mia (*riled now*) You made your choice to stay, Henry. I made mine to leave. It's not my fault she's worse.

Henry (*acid*) And I suppose it's mine.

Beat.

Mia Maybe.

Heavy pause.

Henry I will never forgive you for saying that.

Mia Henry, Jesus, I'm sorry. It's just . . . I've seen you together enough, you know?

Henry She was right about you. You are a little shit.

Pause. Henry makes to leave.

Mia Where are you going?
You're mad.

Henry No. You're mad. If you think he really cares. All he cares about it his peace of mind. He'll have her locked up. On his terms. I can't allow that to happen. I can't.

This won't have been for nothing. This *can't* have been for nothing.

Mia goes to touch him. He pushes her away roughly.

Mia (*hurt*) Henry –

He exits.

SCENE SIX

Early evening of the same day. Martha's flat. Henry's room. The strips of Henry's clothes have gone. Only a few stray ones remain on the floor.

Martha is sitting on the bed. She has had a few drinks. She has the phone and her address book next to her. She plays with the phone receiver. Picking it up and dropping it down. She dials a number, listens then slams the phone down. She flicks through her address book. Chooses another number, dials, waits, no answer, she slams the phone down. She stares into space. Dials again, the talking clock . . .

Martha On the third stroke, the time sponsored by Accurist will be – (*Listens.*) About bloody time . . . (*Laughs.*) Such a nice voice.

She curls up with the receiver in her ear and listens.

On the third stroke.
And forty seconds.
Tock.
Tick-tock.
You have a tremendously lovely voice, don't you know?
(*Extreme mock-posh.*) I was educated at only the finest schools. Played rugger all winter long and learnt to eat the most crumpled crumpets with a silver spoon.

(*Normal voice.*) It is the most tremendously lovely voice. I'm rather jealous.

(*Extreme mock-posh.*) Received pronunciation. Can only be bought. Rather unfashionable, however. Couldn't get a job at the Beeb. Had to become –

(*Normal voice.*) – a talking clock. Dreadful. How dreadful for you. Boy to girl . . .

(*Extreme mock-posh.*) Sir to madam.

(*Normal voice.*) Of course. Sorry. Sir to madam. Is it boring? Because I myself have been looking for work . . .

(*Extreme mock-posh.*) Not a chance, darling. I'm here to stay.

(*Normal voice.*) I see. Thank you. For your . . . time.

She giggles. Hangs up.
Sound of the flat door opening.

Sonia. Not today. Cleaner lady, I told you, not today. I'm busy. Spring cleaning. NO NEED for you. GO AWAY. I am paying myself seven pounds an hour to clean my own hovel. No *need* for you.

She waits for the door to slam shut.
Lurches unsteadily out of bed.

I thought I told you on the phone. There is to be no more cleaning. I am servicing myself just fine . . . in fact I have got a job. A fantastic job. Part of the package includes a cleaner, life insurance, dental care and my own personal scrubber-upper, all on the company.

She has made it to the door.

SONIA! Do I have to tell you to your face?

She swings open the door.

FUCK OFF!

Henry is standing in the doorway. Holding flowers.

Beat.

(*Quieter.*) Fuck off.

She turns and lurches back to bed.

Henry You got a job?

Martha Yes.

Henry What job?

Martha It's in . . . time management.

Henry Seriously?

Martha Yes. I start Monday.

Pause.

Excuse me. Who are you?

Henry Your son, Henry.

He starts rapidly to tidy up the room.

Martha That's funny. I did have a son, called Harry, actually. Well, he died, about five hours ago. I'm a little upset. So if you would just –

Henry Henry. Son called Henry.

Martha Please go and leave me to my grief. You came at a bad time, I was about to have a little ceremony.

Henry puts the flowers in a vase.

Yes. A little ceremony. I was going to burn some of his clothes, you see. To sort of send them up there with him. He liked his clothes. I wouldn't want him to be there without them. (*To the ceiling.*) Can you hear me, Harry dear? He loved his old mum . . .

Do you love your old mum?

Henry I do.

Martha Very much? Because me and Harry – we were close. But you don't have each other for long, mothers and sons, sons and . . . (*Tails off.*) One of you always dies. Way before the other. Hear that, Harry?

You see. You don't have each other for long. So I figured, make the most of it. That's why me and Harry we were so . . . Just making the most of it.

Henry (*collecting glasses*) I see.

Martha Young man.

Henry Yes.

Martha I don't think you do.

Beat.

As it happened you came at a good time. Because. I was going to have this little ceremony, but the thing is, I can't find the clothes to burn. I'm starting to wonder if I didn't just invent little Harry. You see, the only clothes I could find were these.

She picks up some of the scraps of material from the floor.

Henry He must have been small.

Martha Yes. He was. This was his towel.

Henry continues tidying, folding clothes into piles.

Henry I brought you some flowers.

Beat. Henry realises she will only communicate with him if he plays along.

For your loss.

He places them next to the bed.

Martha –

Martha You know, in Africa, when someone dies, they wear white.

Henry I did know that actually, Mummy –

Martha They wear white because they do not believe it to be sad. A death. Not sad at all. Merely part of the bigger . . . journey.

Henry You're wearing white.

She fingers a corner of her nightdress.

Martha This is cream actually.

Henry Mummy –

Still examining her nightdress.

Martha Or is it just dirty? I can't tell any more.

Henry MUMMY!

Pause.

Martha Young man.

Henry Henry. My name's Henry. Come on, please. Dad's landed. He wants to see you. To see us, to see how we are. Help me sort this place out.

Martha Young man.

Henry (*sighs*) At your service.

Gives a little salute.

Martha Hold that pose.

He does.

Has anyone ever told you, you look remarkably like –

Henry A soldier?

Martha Yes. A young soldier. So good.

Drops the salute.

No. Stay like that. It becomes you.

Henry Who am I saluting?

Martha Harry. You are paying your respects to Harry. (*To the ceiling.*) Hear that, boyo?

Henry To Harry. Wise son. (*Mutters.*) The one who got away.

Henry salutes the ceiling. Then snaps back into clearing up.

Did you really get a job?

Martha Let me check.

She dials 123, listens to the speaking clock for a split second.

No vacancies.

Henry You could. Get a job. It would be good for you. Get you out of the house. Get you out of this – (*Gestures at the bed.*)

Martha I don't need one. Other people need one more then me. If I took a job there would be one less for the proletariat. It would be against my principles.

Henry Of course. You've never had one.

Martha That's not true – when I was at art college I used to go fruit picking in the summer. It was nice for the first few days, the sun, all the apples you could eat, but after one month I hated it. I still won't drink apple juice.

Henry (*quietly*) Maybe it would have been better for all of us if you had worked in a vineyard.
What have you done today?
Have you got up since I left this morning?

She shrugs.

Say something.

Martha (*slurs*) Soldier.

Henry You're pissed.

Martha laughs.

You need food.

He exits to the kitchen.
   While he is gone Martha takes the flowers and removes the petals. She sprinkles them over the bed.
   Henry re-enters with tears in his eyes and an open can in his hand.

Have you been eating this?

Martha nods her head.

When. When did you eat this?

She laughs.

Mummy. Martha. (*Getting upset.*) This isn't funny.

Beat.

This is cat food.

She mock-miaows.

Martha Come here. Onto my bed of roses, soldier. Come here.

Henry This – (*Gestures around the room.*) This. This is over.

Martha Come here.

Henry No. Daddy is coming back. Do you not understand? He's coming back. And if I don't sort you –

Martha Come here.

Henry NO.
(*To himself*.) I'm a fool.

Martha You're a soldier –

Henry I thought there was maybe a sneaking chance, the tiniest chance that if I came back today, that you might, *just might*, have attempted to pull yourself together. So Dad won't realise what a mess you are. That you would be a little sad, maybe. A little rough around the edges as normal. But OK. Trying to be OK. That you would at least try to help me help us.

Beat.

I'm a fucking fool.

Martha Don't swear.

Pause.

Henry Were you really eating cat food? Or did you just want me to think so?
I'll never know.

Martha sits up on the bed. She shakes her head, looks as if she's visibly trying to pull herself together, trying to sober up.

I thought we could bluff this. Convince him I had it under control. Tidy up, sober you up. Stupid. Stupid. Stupid me.

Pause.

Will you go? With me? Will you go with me today, to a clinic? Will you check yourself in?

Martha (*trying hard to sound sober*) The cat food, it was –

Henry WILL YOU GO WITH ME TODAY?

Pause.

Martha The cat food. It was for the strays. I didn't –

Henry WILL YOU GO WITH ME TODAY?

Martha I DIDN'T EAT IT.

Henry Too late.

Beat.

You can come with me today. You can choose the place.
It will be private. Comfortable. Or. You can wait for Dad
who, if he sees you like this – if he believes Mia, if he
believes you are a danger to us, to yourself – will have
you taken away.

Beat.

Choose.

Martha (*quietly*) I didn't eat it.

Henry Will you go?

Martha No. Sorry. No.

Henry Do it for me.

Martha No.

Henry So I can go, and know you're safe. So I can look
Dad in the eye when he comes. So I can know that I helped
you somehow. Please. This one thing. (*Urgently.*) I don't
want you to get sectioned. I won't be able to visit you.
It'll be like before, remember? I don't know where they'll
take you. I don't know if they'll let you out.

Beat.

If you volunteer yourself, if you come with me, then you
can leave. Then you can choose. Please. Please.

I'm fucking begging you.

Martha I'll go. I'll go if –

66

Henry If what?

Martha If you have a drink with me.

SCENE SEVEN

Late that evening. A restaurant. Mia and Hugh are sitting together. There are a bottle of wine and a bottle of water on the table and two menus.

Mia is fiddling with her napkin. They sit in silence for some moments.

Hugh clears his throat. Mia looks up. He says nothing. She looks back down at her napkin.

Hugh It's a nice –

Mia Restaurant.

Hugh Yes. Nice place. Good steak. Can't get a good steak in Hong Kong.

Mia Really?

Hugh Well. Some of the grander hotels. But it's very expensive. So. Not really. No.

Mia Oh.

Hugh Are you hungry?

Mia Yeah.

Hugh What's the school food like?

Mia Terrible.

Hugh Mine was awful. Blood sausage, suet pudding.

Mia Ugh.

Silence.

Hugh Do you want a glass of wine?

Mia No.

Hugh A beer?

Mia Water is fine.

Hugh OK. Sure.

Silence. He pours her a glass of water.

Well. I thought that went well. Considering.

Pause.

They'll take you back. That's the main thing. A few new digital cameras . . . Couldn't have managed a whole wing now, could we?

Mia nods.

I didn't like my boarding school much. You're not meant to like it much. It's a passport really. For your future –

Mia For my future.

Hugh You understand.

Beat.

So. Tomorrow –

Mia I think I will have some wine, actually.

Hugh OK.

He pours her a glass.

We'll go round there. Early. Henry will be at school, you can get your things. I can –

She is fiddling with her fork.

Mia Is this real silver?

Hugh examines it.

Hugh No. Heavy though. Listen, I –

Mia You look tanned.

Hugh Do I?

Mia Yeah.

Hugh You should come out and visit. See your baby sister.

Mia Are there beaches?

Hugh Some. I live on a hill.

Mia I thought –

Hugh We moved. Needed more room. For the baby.

Mia Oh.

Pause.

Is it hot there all the time?

Hugh More muggy, really. Sweaty weather.

Mia They say it's going to be a hot summer here.

Hugh That will be nice.

Mia Global warming.

Hugh At least you'll get tanned.

Mia Like you?

Hugh You could come out, you know. I'd like you to come out. We all would.

Mia Henry too?

Hugh Henry too.

Pause. Hugh examines the menu.

This place has changed. More expensive. Are you starving?

Mia It's only been a minute.

Hugh I'm starving.

Mia You asked me that.

Hugh I did.

Beat.

Listen, Mia –

Mia I think these *are* real silver, you know. They have a mark and everything.

Hugh Tomorrow. I want to avoid a scene.

Mia A tiny mark, look.

She hands the fork to him. He takes her hand in his and puts it down on the table.

Hugh Mia –

Mia You're sweating. Brought the sweaty weather with you?

He wipes his palm on his trousers.

Hugh Mia –

Mia What?

Hugh I need you to fill me in.

Mia Thought the school filled you in.

Hugh They told me what they thought.

Mia Super.

Hugh I need you to tell me about Martha.

Mia She was your wife. You know her better then I do.

Hugh Don't.

Mia Don't what?

Hugh Just co-operate. OK?

Mia OK.

Hugh You're not getting on. Is that it?

Mia You could say that.

Hugh She's drinking again.

Mia nods.

The pills?

Mia Are nothing new. Lots of people take them. Have you read *Prozac Nation*?

Hugh She's – misusing the pills? Is that it?

Mia shrugs.

Mia. I need to know as much as you can tell me before I see her.

Mia Why?

Hugh So I can be prepared.

Mia What do you actually do?

Hugh Excuse me?

Mia At work these days. I'm never sure.

Hugh That's not the point.

Mia I'm interested.

Hugh I'm a broker. You know that.

Mia You broker deals and things?

Hugh Yes. Deals and things.

Mia So you have skills?

Hugh I suppose so. Listen, this isn't what this is about. We can talk about my work another time. Let's get back on topic.

Mia Back on topic? (*Snorts.*) OK. Broker a deal tomorrow. I don't know – bribe her or something. You don't need my help. You don't need *preparation*. You're great at your job. You love it.

Hugh Mia, if you don't explain the situation I won't be able to solve it

Mia It's not Sudoku, Dad.

Hugh (*sighs*) I know, but what's the story?

Mia It's not mine to tell. It's Henry's.

Hugh How is he?

Mia What do you think?

Hugh I –

Mia Don't know, do you?

Hugh Jesus.

Mia Can I smoke?

Hugh No. You bloody can't.

Mia I'll go outside?

Hugh No.

Mia Fine.

Hugh Since when did you smoke?

Mia Since when did you care?

Hugh When did you start?

Mia I was considering starting tonight.

Hugh Is this all I get?

Mia Pardon?

Hugh This. You should be grateful.

Silence.

Mia?

Beat.

Mia. They were going to expel you. I got you out of it.
Understand? You have no respect.

Mia Do you?

Pause.

Hugh What you did was unacceptable. I don't want to
go on about it. But you are not in a position to be getting
cheeky, young lady. Not in a position at all.
    So would you please co-operate?

Beat.

OK?

Heavy pause.

Now, tell me what to expect. Properly.

Mia appears to be considering her options.

Mia They're fine, Dad. She just got a bit pissed that
night. That's all.

Hugh That's all?

Mia Sure.

Hugh That's not what the school think.

Mia They're just tense about being sued, hyper-vigilant
etcetera.
    It'll be fine tomorrow. Henry will be at school. You
can talk to her alone. Make up your own mind.

73

Hugh I think a clinic is best, don't you? Clean her up a bit. You might not think it's necessary. We can arrange it tonight. I think the school would appreciate that.

Mia Like I said. It was just a wobble. She's all right, really. In fact, I'd say she's practically better.

Hugh There are people you can pay to ensure that. Takes the pressure off.

He spots the food coming.

Ah, here it comes. Finally, proper steak.

SCENE EIGHT

Around nine in the morning. Henry's room.
Henry and Martha have been up all night. Henry has been drinking with Martha, trying to convince her to go. She has been playing games with him and seems to be ignoring his plans for departure. She has dressed him up in her nightdress and dressed herself in an evening gown. Henry is urgently trying to dress Martha more sensibly in preparation to leave.

Martha Jewels, I must have jewels. Where are my jewels?

She swigs from her nearly empty glass.

Under the bed. I hid them there. I hid them from thieves. Who wants my jewels? Everybody wants my jewels. That, what's her name, Sonia. She wanted my jewels.

Henry takes the glass from her.

Oh don't be a bore.

Henry tries to put a cardigan on her. She shrugs it off.

Fetch my jewels, soldier.

Henry You need to change. Put this on.

74

Martha Fine. I'll fetch them.

Martha reaches under the bed and pulls out a large jewellery box.

Look at you. God. You should have been a girl. You would have been a beautiful girl. Look at you.

She starts rummaging around in the jewellery box, plucking out items and holding them against Henry's face. She starts trying to put a necklace on him.

Henry Don't. We need to leave.

Martha Just let me see.

She adjusts it around his neck.

So pretty. I'll wear matching.

She starts putting more jewellery on herself and Henry.

Henry Get dressed.

Henry tries to put shoes on her. She kicks him away playfully and giggles.

Martha Only a glass slipper will fit . . .

Henry keeps trying to put the shoes on her feet. While his head is at her waist level she hoops more necklaces over his neck.

War spoils for my soldier. He glitters. Look how he glitters.

She kisses his face.
He has managed to get the shoes on. He stands, finds the cardigan and holds it for her to put on.

Henry Put it on.

Martha You haven't touched your drink.

Henry I don't want it.

Martha Let's have a toast.

She raises her glass.

Henry Now. We need to leave now.

Martha A toast to. A toast to –

Henry tries to put the cardigan on her again. She shrugs him off and stands.

Let's have a toast. Come on.

Henry Just let me –

Martha With your old mum. Come on.

She kicks off the shoes.

Henry Jesus . . .

Martha A toast, to my son, so good . . .

Martha drains the glass and hands it to him.

Henry Now, you promised. Let's go.

Martha Finish yours. It's rude – there was a toast to you and you didn't drink.

Henry Then we'll go?

Martha These are ugly shoes. You can always tell the quality of a person by their shoes. Their shoes and their haircut . . . and perhaps their jewellery. I have nice jewels, don't I . . . Pretty things.

Beat.

Finish it.

He sits down on the edge of the bed and takes his glass. It is obvious he really doesn't want it, but he downs it. Martha giggles in delight. She kisses his face. While she's doing this he slings the cardigan round her shoulders. He tries unsuccessfully to pull her up.

Henry We'll get a taxi.

Martha (*giggling*) Look at you.

Henry I'll change on the way.

The door buzzes.
  Martha continues kissing Henry's face.

Who is that?

Martha Sonia.

Henry It's not –

Martha Too early. Must be Sonia. Come to help you clean up.

Door buzzes again.

Hide the jewels. She always tries to steal from me. Hide them.

Martha heads to the exit to answer the door.
  She exits.
  Panicked, Henry clumsily picks up the jewellery box and shoves it under the bed. Some of the contents have spilled out onto the floor. He shovels them under the bed.
  It is in this position, on his hands and knees that Hugh and Mia first see him, as they enter with Martha behind them.
  Silence. Henry stands up.

Martha Daddy's here.

Henry You're early.

Hugh takes in the room.

Hugh Pyjamas in the wash?

Henry You're too early.

They all look at him for a moment.

I feel sick.

Martha Baby . . .

Henry Just looking at him. I feel sick.

Hugh Why don't you go and get dressed, Henry?

Henry Don't you like my new look?

Hugh Go and get some clothes on. Get your stuff for school. Mia, pack yourself a few things too.

Pause.

Henry You're amazing.

Mia Come on, Hen.

Henry Actually amazing.

Mia Come on, leave them to it.

Hugh I want a word with Martha alone.

Henry I don't think she wants to be alone with you, do you?

Hugh Come on, Henry. Just do what you're told.

Henry Amazing.

Mia Let's get our stuff together.

Henry Mummy?

Martha (*almost to herself*) Daddy's really here . . .

Mia And aren't you dressed for the occasion?

Martha Henry, baby, I need some coffee, will you go and make me some, darling?

Henry Mia can do it.

Martha You know just how I like it.

Mia I'll help you.

Henry walks over to Hugh and sniffs him.

Henry You reek of duty-free.

Henry exits. Mia follows.

Hugh He always gives me that look. Even when he was two. It's sinister.

Hugh bends down and picks up a stray necklace from the floor. He holds it in his hands as if weighing it.

Martha You gave me all of this. Remember. All of this –

Beat.

– tinsel.

Hugh gently rests the necklace he was holding on the side table.

Hugh This place is a mess.

Martha I sacked my cleaner.
How's slinky-eyes?

Hugh Why was Henry dressed like that? In your necklace?

Martha shrugs.
Hugh runs his finger over a surface.

This place is filthy.

He notices the bottles. He sighs.
He sits down.

Hugh What's going on, Martha?

Martha You tell me, smarty pants. Its not often family number one merit a transpacific visit.

She starts frantically rummaging for a cigarette.

Hugh What are you looking for?

Martha A fag –

As she says this she knocks something over. It smashes.

Hugh You're drunk.

Martha Where are my fucking cigarettes?

She stands.

Hugh Martha. Sit down.

Martha (*mocking him*) Hugh, stand up.

Hugh We need to talk.

Hugh goes over to her and tries to guide her back down.

Down you go.

Martha curls up on the bed. She buries herself deeper in the bed. Hugh comes closer. He gently pulls her up off the bed.

Look at me.

She stares at him.

I'm going to take you to the Cromwell. I'll pay for it, I've arranged it . . .

Beat.

You're not well.

Martha reaches out and touches his face.

Don't.

She rests her head on his shoulder. He is uncomfortable with it, but allows her to.

They sit still like this for a moment. Martha then smells him.

Martha Duty-free . . . delicious.

Beat.

Did you bring me a present?

Hugh What?

Martha Always used to. Pockets full of presents. Cold lips from being outside. Warm mouth. The taxi door slamming.

Hugh I never slammed the door.

Martha Yes, you did. Slammed it and pounded up the stairs. You did. I remember.

Hugh I didn't –

Martha Bring me a present? Yes you did. You're hiding it.

Beat.

In one of your pockets. Something from the east. Something dinky.

Hugh Martha. I just didn't. I didn't even get the kids one.

Martha But you always do.

Hugh Did. Always did.

Beat.

Martha Tight bastard.

Hugh Don't.

Martha Bet you got her one.

Hugh Not now.

Martha Exotic toys for your exotic toy.

Hugh This is not about her.

Martha Is it true, what they say?

Hugh No.

Martha You don't know what I'm about to say.

Hugh I don't want to.

Henry reappears in the doorway. They don't see him.

Martha Worried I'm going to be rude?

Beat.

Worried I'm going to be *vulgar* . . .

Beat.

Because you don't like that, do you, Hugh? That's why you married a third-rate geisha. (*Sexily and slowly.*) Total obedience . . .

Martha leans forward as if to kiss him. He springs back.

Hugh Don't.

Martha (*snarls*) As if.

Henry Jingle bells, jingle bells, jingle all the way. Oh what fun it is to run . . .

Mia enters.

What? It must be Christmas time surely? All of us together in one room. Oh no. I forgot. We don't even do that at Christmas.

Hugh Mia, take Henry to get changed, then walk him to school. It's after nine.

Silence.

I'll pick you up after. We'll talk then. Right now I need to deal with Martha. Off you go. You'll be late.

Henry You didn't tell him?

Mia shakes her head.

You don't know the fucking half of it, do you, Dad? I don't go to school any more. I dropped out. About a year and a half ago, actually.

Henry laughs, a little giddy with his own outburst.

Hugh (*to Mia*) Did you know about this?

Mia nods.

Henry Thought you might have noticed when the fees stopped plopping out of your account every three months. Clearly not.

Hugh Why wasn't I told?

Martha You didn't ask.

Hugh I didn't ask because I take it on assumption that my children attend school like every other normal teenager in the country.
A year and a half ago?

Henry nods.

And what, may I ask, have you been doing since then?

Henry What do you think?

Hugh I don't know, Henry. I have no idea.

Martha He's been at home with me.

Hugh Here? In this fetid bedroom?

I've been teaching him art.

Henry Look.

He shoves a handful of drawings at Hugh.

Hugh Sketching?

Martha He's good at it.

Mia starts to laugh.

Hugh Why are you laughing?

Mia It's just funny, that's all. Your face.

Henry starts to laugh as well.

Henry You've gone red.

Hugh IT IS NOT FUCKING FUNNY.

Pause. Martha giggles.

You tell me, Martha, what the hell is going on, because this has a nightmarish quality I don't like.

Martha Nightmarish quality you don't like? I really am very very sorry about that, Hugh. That you don't like it. That it doesn't suit you. Because you see, darling, you relinquished parental responsibility when you fucked off with your little strumpet.

Hugh I had to go around to that school and beg them to the point of blackmail to keep her there. They tell me she never stays here, that there isn't enough room –

Martha THERE ISN'T ENOUGH ROOM FOR THREE, THERE ISN'T ENOUGH MONEY FOR THREE.

Hugh Money? You want money?

Martha Look at how we live, while you – you shack up in some palace in the sun with that woman. Probably got servants. Look at this hole. This filthy little hole. There isn't enough room for your children.

Mia Hen. Let's go. Let's leave them to it.

Henry Gee, Daddy. You look tanned.

Martha Off you go, Missy. Of you go with your pa. Me and Henry. Staying right here.

Henry Climate must suit you.

Martha Come here, baby.

Hugh Go get yourself some breakfast, here –

He proffers some money.

Henry (*mocking him*) 'Money? You want money?'

Martha (*to Mia*) Off you trot, Missy.

She waves her hand in a dismissive gesture at Mia.

Mia Don't tell me what to do.

Martha Piss off now, thank you.

Mia Henry, come with me.

Henry I'm not leaving her with him.

Mia Please.

Martha Always interrupting.

Mia I'm going to get you – I'm going to fucking get you.

Hugh Mia –

Martha I want my son.

She stumbles towards Henry.
Mia shoves Martha back on the bed.

Did you see that? Did you see that? She's gone wild. Hurting me. Lying to me. *Stealing* from me.

Mia (*seething*) You haven't seen wild.

Martha Your daughter, stealing from me. I want my son. HENRY, HENRY!

Mia Leave. Him. Alone.

They are fighting now.

Hugh STOP IT!

Pause.

Mia You heartless cunt.

Hugh MIA!

Mia Don't shout at me.

Hugh I know this is very emotional –

Mia How the fuck would you know how emotional it is?
You weren't there, you didn't see –

Hugh Mia, please. That's hardly helping –

Martha Oooh, Daddio's in trouble now.

Mia SHUT UP!

Beat.

Go on then.

Beat.

Daddio.

Hugh Martha. I'm taking you to the clinic. If you won't
go voluntarily, I'll . . . you know what I can do.

Beat.

Martha Are you threatening me? (*To Mia.*) He's
threatening me – he's flown all the way over to do what
he likes best. Don't be under any illusions, sweetie, your
daddy doesn't give a fuck about you. He's just a tidy
man. Used to fold his own underwear. He's a tidy man
trying to tidy me away and tidy you both up. Not for
you. For him. Don't be fooled, little madam. Your
daddy's no hero. Threatening me –

Henry stands up.

Hugh Henry. Sit down, you look ridiculous. Martha,
I am not threatening you. I am making you aware of your
options.

Martha You could have threatened me over the phone,
Hughie. Saved yourself the – (*Spits the word.*) air miles.

Hugh Then you leave me no choice.

Martha But that choice suits you, Hughie. Doesn't it?
It's cheaper to have me sectioned, isn't it? It's not private.
You want me in an NHS loony bin 'cause it won't cost
you a pretty penny. Did he tell you that I called him?
That I asked for his help? I couldn't afford a clinic
without him. He just wanted it to come to this. I bet he
didn't tell you that in your little heart-to-heart. Don't be
fooled, sweetie. He's been waiting for this.

Mia Is this true?

Hugh Of course not.

Martha He sat in the sun and waited. Till he could
polish me off at the expense of the taxpayer. Money's
bound to be tight now, eh? With family number two. Bet
young slinky-eyes is developing expensive tastes –

Mia Did she call you?

Martha Look at her. Tell her the truth.

Hugh Your mother is a very sick woman, Mia. But I
promise you, I thought –

Mia What did you think?

Hugh I thought what you told me last night was true –

Martha Do you think he didn't know? Petal, we're just a
mess to him. You're just a mess to him.

Hugh Of course not, Mia. We've talked about this –

Martha He knew.

Mia When you stopped hearing from us. When you stopped getting Henry's school reports. Why didn't you call? Why didn't you check?

Hugh I thought you were OK.

Mia You wanted to think we were OK.

Martha He didn't give a shit.

Hugh Why would I be here if I didn't?

Mia So you don't have your good name sullied because your daughter was taken into care.

Beat.

That's the real reason, isn't it?

Hugh Mia –

Mia Isn't it?

Martha See him properly. Go on. See what he is.

Mia stares at Hugh.

Mia You could have stopped all of this. But you left. And she was sick when you left. But you left us anyway.

Hugh When you're older –

Mia You won't know me when I'm older.

Martha Good girl.

Mother and daughter stare at each other for a second.

We don't need him, do we? It's too late for him.

Beat.

Come and sit next to me.

Mia does nothing. She looks as if she's about to cry.

Next to me and Henry. Come on.

88

Mia is clearly wavering.

Mia (*quietly*) Henry. I want to go.

Henry stands up.

Henry What do you reckon of me? Have I grown?

Mia (*sobbing*) Please, Henry.

Henry Practically your height now. Though you never were a tall bloke.

Mia (*crying now*) NOW!

Hugh Take her outside, Henry.

Henry Was that an order, sir?

Martha mock-salutes.

I'm not going anywhere. This is not your problem. It is not your house. This isn't even your fucking continent any more. I had things going just fine before you barged in.

Hugh I have flown halfway across the world to help you sort out this . . . Do you think this is my idea of a splendid morning? I thought you were at school. I thought you were better than this.

Henry Oh Daddy Bear, have we surprised you?

Hugh I know you're angry with me. I know I haven't been perfect. I know that. But right now I am trying to get this resolved. This is why I wanted you to go away to school. This is why. But you didn't want to. I should have made you. Look at you . . . Christ.

Mia (*under her breath*) Too late.

Hugh If you want to help her, we have to work together, as a team. OK?

Silence.

OK?

Silence.

Mia. I'll call a taxi. You shouldn't have to see this.

Mia (*sobbing*) Not. Without. Henry.

Hugh Leave me with Martha. I'll deal with her.

Henry You're not coming anywhere near her. I'm dealing with her.

Mia No.

Martha He's staying here with me. Aren't you, Henry?

Mia Be my big brother and take me out of this. Please.

Henry Go if you want. Go home with team Daddio.

Mia Henry, I didn't tell him. I didn't tell him anything. I did what you wanted, this isn't my fault. I'm sorry about what I said.

Henry I had it under control.

He goes to Martha on the bed. She snuggles up to him, Martha smiles to Mia and Hugh.

Hugh Get up, Henry.

Martha snuggles deeper into Henry. She whispers to him.

I'VE HAD ENOUGH.

Henry springs up.

Henry Had enough, have you? Had e-fucking-nough? Of what, Hugh? Had enough of what? Papa Bear is in a tizz now, ain't he? Look at him. You've gone red, sir.

Martha giggles.

Hugh You don't have a choice. She's going.

Henry No. You can't just do that. You can't just. Come. Here. In your chinos. With. Your. Solution. You can't do that. It's. Just. Not. Right.

Pause.

'Cause, you see – (*Spits the word.*) Daddy, you left me here all by myself. So I did what I thought you should have done. Taken care of her. Taken very good care of her. Like she was broken. 'Cept I thought I could fix her. Thought I'd do anything to fix her. Used to wish it on eyelashes.

Hugh Henry –

Henry You're. Not. Right. You can't just do that. It pisses on me. You're pissing on me.

He stands on the bed, swaying slightly.

Martha Sit down. Come down. Baby boy. Come here.

He kicks her away.

Henry None of you understand. Do you? None of you. Five years. I've tried. And tried. None of you fucking understand. Anything. About it. All the blood she's kicked. From. My. Heart. And now you piss on me too. You piss on all I've done. I might as well piss on me.

Looks down at himself.

Would that scare you, Hugh? Would that scare you away? You don't like things to crazy, do you, Daddy? DO YOU? They make you run away.

He pisses himself. They are stunned.

Hugh Jesus.

Martha Sit down. Next to me. Henry. Baby.

Henry Stupid me.

He is standing on the bed. Martha tries to pull him down. Henry turns on her.

You. You promised I would be the one to have got you to go. One thing. One thing for me. So I could know that I helped you, so I could know it wasn't a terrible mistake, all that trying and crying and trying for you. And you wouldn't. After one drink. After another drink. And you wouldn't, all night you wouldn't. Of course you wouldn't. Should have known. Trapped us here so he could see how bad we'd got. News flash. He doesn't fucking care. I care. Setting a trap for your beautiful boy. Your beautiful baby. Well, how's your soldier boy now, Mummy? HOW'S YOUR SOLDIER BOY NOW?

Stunned silence.
Martha stands and lifts her arms to Henry as if to help him down.

Mia They're going to come and take her. You don't want to see that.

Henry Belong here. I belong here. Leave us be –

Mia I won't leave you here.

Hugh You did what you could, Henry. You're a good boy – (*Sighs.*) to bad parents. But it's over now. It really is over now.

Henry shakes his head again and again and again.
Henry's outburst and the state of him has shocked Martha. It seems as though only now has she realised the destruction she has caused.
Martha says nothing but stares at Henry, who is shaking his head over and over.

Martha.

Martha continues staring at Henry.

Look at me.

She does.
   He fishes his mobile out of his pocket.

I am calling them now.

   He dials.

Martha No.

Hugh You have no choice.

Martha No.

   Beat.

I'll go.

   On this Henry lurches up.

Henry No. No. No. You can't go. You can't go. No.

   He crawls to her and wraps his arms around her legs.

Can't leave me. Stay with me. Belong together. Here, we
belong here. You're lying – you're lying to make them
go away. Fit for you. We fit together. Please, Mummy.
Mummy, please. Stay. Stay with me. I'll lie to the doctors,
I'll say she made it up. If you stay, things will be OK. I'm
yours I'm yours I'm yours . . . what you wanted. Me.
Yours.

   She tries to gently disentangle herself from him.
   *Henry is groping up her body with his arms, burying
his face in her tummy, clinging to her, shaking his head
over and over.*

Gave you what you wanted. This is what you wanted.
I chose you. Choose me back, choose me back.

   Martha is still, staring down at Henry.

Hugh I'm calling now.

Henry Choose me back.

Martha Don't.

Beat.

I don't want him to see me taken.

Mia Then fucking leave.

Martha runs her hands through Henry's hair, soothing him.

Martha (*murmurs softly*) Baby boy, baby boy, don't cry.

He is soothed and starts just to cling to her. She lifts his face up with her hand. They are now looking at each other.

Am I a lady?

Henry nods.

Your lady?

Henry nods.

A lady can't be taken away. A lady must have dignity. A lady must go . . . herself. If I don't go, they'll take me. To a bad place. I won't be able to see you. And I want to see you. I want to see that face. My baby's face.

Beat.

I was so happy when I was pregnant with you. It was the happiest time of my life. I felt clear. Everything felt clear. With you inside me. Everything fell away.

Beat.

(*Very softly.*) This way we have each other for ever. This way, I'll always have you in here – (*She touches her lower stomach.*) We own each other. No one can take it away, Henry. No one.

Beat.

But I have to go now. I have to go away.

Beat.

Let go.

He clings harder.

Always here – (*Touches her belly.*)

Mia Let go.

She gently disentangles herself from him.

Are you my soldier? My own soldier?

He nods.

Then be brave.

He lets go of her.
She takes her handbag, looks around the room, at Hugh, at Mia. She opens her mouth as if to say something, but doesn't.
Slowly, with twisted dignity, she exits.
The door is heard shutting behind her.
Henry has his head in his hands on the floor. Mia is standing, stunned. Hugh follows Martha offstage. They say nothing for some moments.
Mia turns to Henry.
Henry looks up and meets her eyes, yet says nothing.

Mia It's OK. I promise. It's OK. We're OK.

The scene stays like this for a moment, the only sound being Henry's jagged breaths.
Lights fade to black.

The End.

Acknowledgements

I wish to thank everyone at the YWP
and the staff of the Royal Court Theatre

Particular thanks to Lyndsey Turner,
Dominic Cooke and Jeremy Herrin
for all their insight, support and criticism.
Thanks also to Team Deathbat
for all their loving support, most notably
Penny, Nutty, Alex, Maia, Hamish, Joe,
Daisy and Johnny Lloyd (who read it first)